SCHIRMER'S LIBRARY
OF MUSICAL CLASSICS

Vol. 2037

Dmitri Kabalevsky

Easy Pieces

24 Pieces for Children, Op. 39
35 Easy Pieces, Op. 89

For Piano

Boosey & Hawkes Music Publishers Ltd.
Sole Selling Agents of Anglo-Soviet Music Press, London
for Great Britain, Eire and the British Commonwealth (except Canada)

Le Chant du Monde, Paris
pour la France, Belgique, Luxembourg et les pays francophones de l'Afrique

Edition Fazer, Helsinki
for Finland

G. Ricordi & C. Milano
per l'Italia

Musikverlag Hans Sikorski, Hamburg
für Deutschland, Dänemark, Island, Norwegen,
Schweden, Niederlande, Schweiz, Spanien, Portugal, Griechland, Türkei und Israel

Univeral Edition A.G., Wien
für Österriech

Zen-On Music Company Ltd., Tokyo
for Japan

ISBN 978-0-7935-8930-2

G. SCHIRMER, Inc.

DISTRIBUTED BY

HAL•LEONARD®
CORPORATION
7777 W. BLUEMOUND RD. P.O. BOX 13819 MILWAUKEE, WI 53213

24 PIECES FOR CHILDREN

1 Melody

Dmitri Kabalevsky, Op. 39

2 Polka

3 Rambling

4 Cradle Song

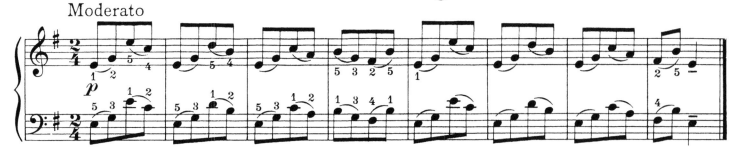

5 Playing

6 A Little Joke

7 Funny Event

8 Song

9 A Little Dance

10 March

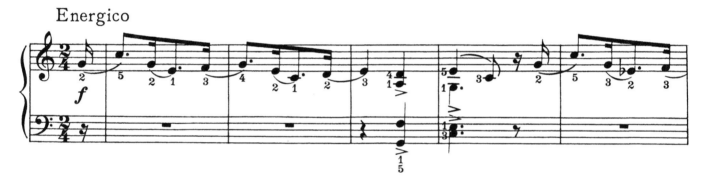

11 Song of Autumn

Andante cantabile

12 Scherzo

Vivo, giocoso

13 Waltz

8

14 A Fable

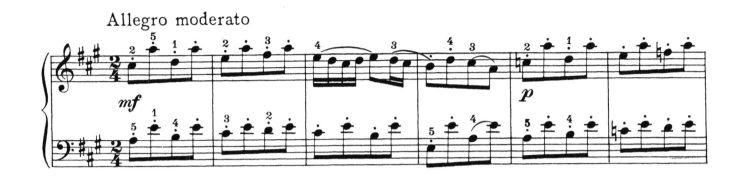

15 Jumping

16 A Sad Story

17 Folk Dance

18 Galop

19 Prelude

20 Clowns

21 Improvisation

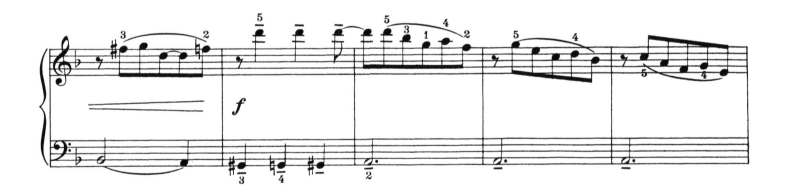

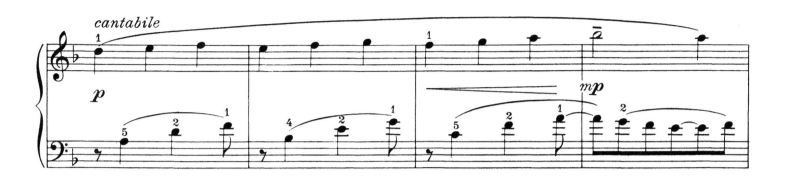

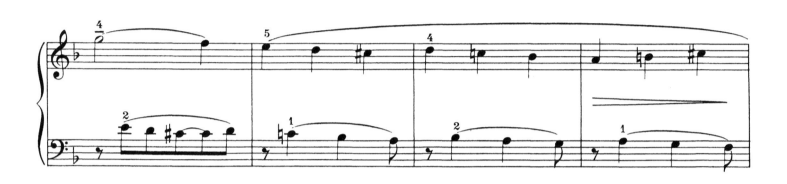

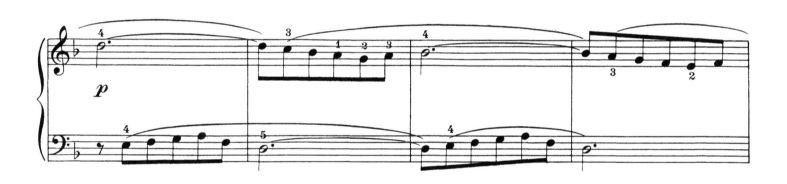

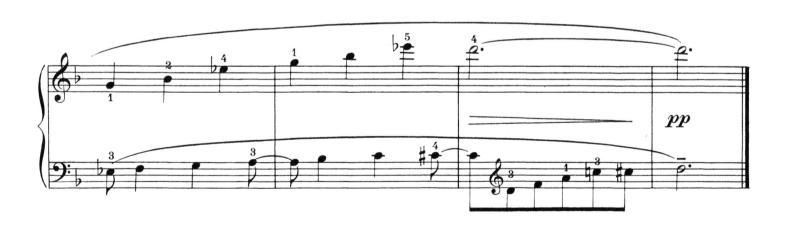

22 A Short Story

23 Slow Waltz

24 A Happy Outing

Resoluto con brio

35 EASY PIECES
Op. 89 (1972)

1
First Piece

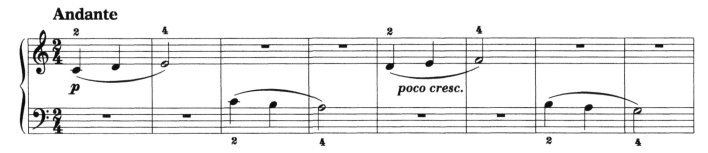

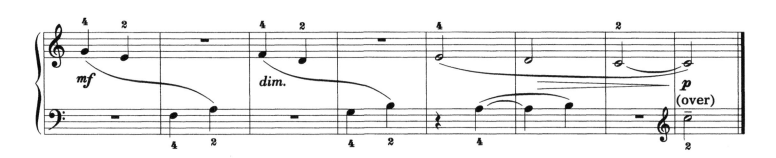

2
First Etude

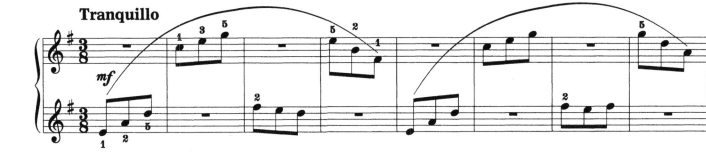

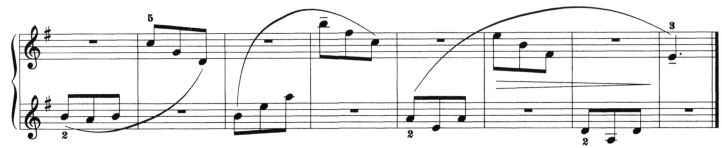

3
Quiet Song

4
At Recess

5
First Waltz

6
The Jumping Champion

7
Light and Shadow

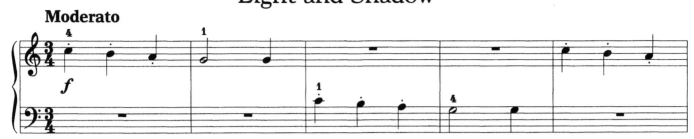

8
Little Hedgehog

9
Song in Octaves

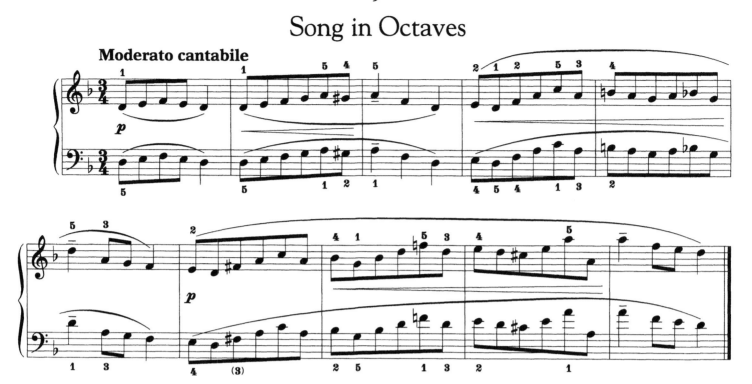

10
Playful One

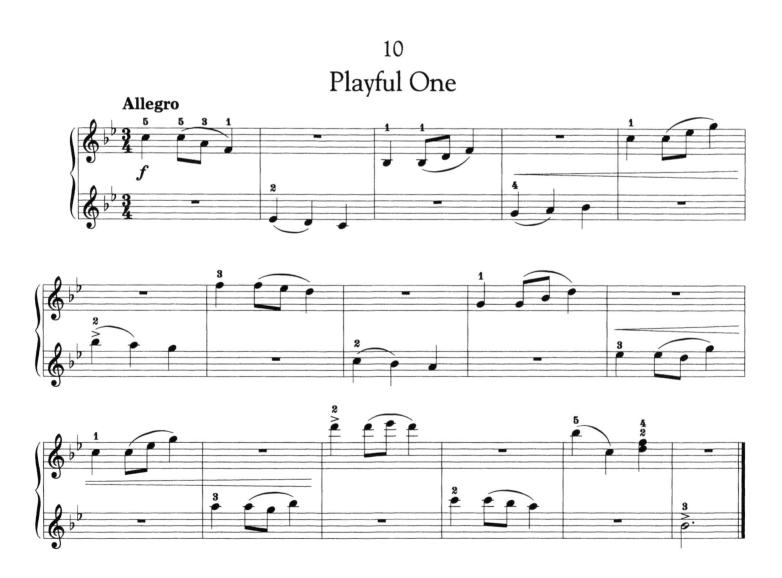

11
Crybaby

12
The Shrew

13
Soothing Song

14
Morning Song

15
Trumpet and Echo

16
Evening Song

17
Skipping Rope

18

On the Ice

19

Little Goat Limping

20
Trumpet and Drum

Marziale

21
The Little Juggler

22
March

23
Brave Song

24
The Little Harpist

25
Chastushka*

* The Russian *chastushka* is a short humorous verse that satirizes or pokes fun at something, similar in spirit to the English *limerick*. —Editors

26
A Merry Game

27
Stubborn Little Brother

28

Buratino's Dance

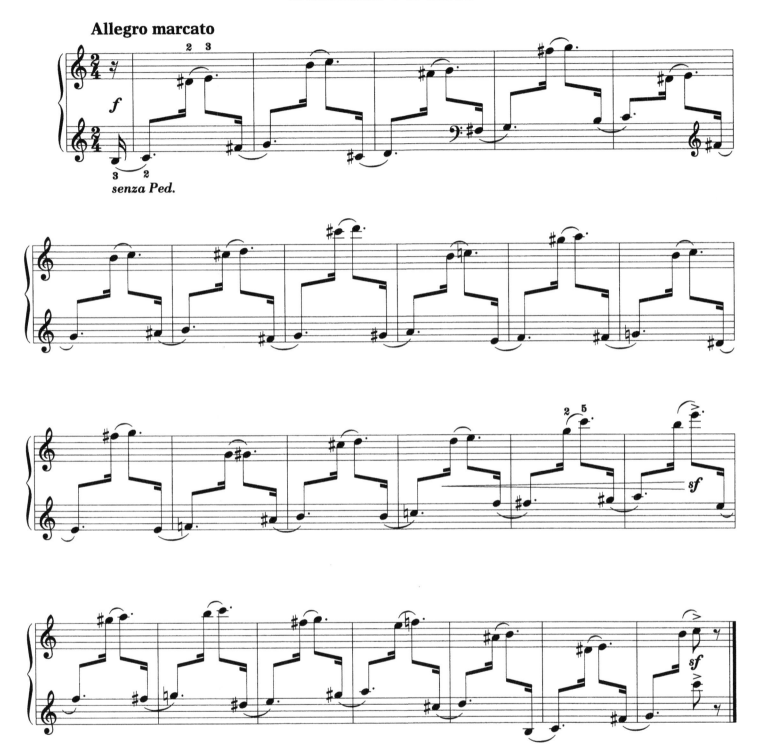

29
Melody

Tranquillo, cantabile

tenuto con Ped.

30
Fighting Song

Rabbit Teasing a Bear-Cub

32
Little Hippo Dance

33
Almost a Waltz

34
Melancholy Rain

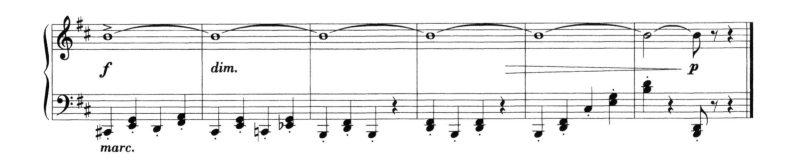

35
By the Water